VIKING EXPLORERS

First European Voyagers to North America

HENRIETTA TOTH

ROSEN
PUBLISHING®

New York

For my niece Emi, who likes to explore new places

Published in 2017 by The Rosen Publishing Group, Inc.
29 East 21st Street, New York, NY 10010

Copyright © 2017 by The Rosen Publishing Group, Inc.

First Edition

Library of Congress Cataloging-in-Publication Data

Names: Toth, Henrietta, author.
Title: Viking explorers : first European voyagers to North America / Henrietta Toth.
Description: First edition. | New York : Rosen Publishing, 2017. | Series: Spotlight on explorers and colonization | Includes bibliographical references and index.
Identifiers: LCCN 2015051135| ISBN 9781477788349 (library bound) | ISBN 9781477788325 (pbk.) | ISBN 9781477788332 (6-pack)
Subjects: LCSH: Vikings--Juvenile literature. | Northmen--Juvenile literature. | Civilization, Viking--Juvenile literature.
Classification: LCC DL66 .T68 2017 | DDC 948/.022--dc23
LC record available at http://lccn.loc.gov/2015051135

Manufactured in the United States of America

CONTENTS

WHO WERE THE VIKINGS?

The Vikings were Norse people who lived in the northern European countries known today as Scandinavia. They came to be called Vikings during the late eighth century to the early eleventh century because of their seafaring raids on other countries. The Vikings were famous for being pirates, warriors, slavers, and marauding barbarians. However, they were also traders, explorers, settlers, farmers, and skilled craftsmen.

Viking people lived in tribes that were organized according to their locations. These tribes were spread out far and wide. Sometimes they fought against each other. There was no central ruling government. Instead, a chieftain led each tribe.

Yet, all Vikings shared a similar way of life. Most Vikings lived on small farms. Some farms were near each other, while others were isolated. Mainly cows and sheep were raised for meat and dairy products like milk and cheese. Hay was grown to feed the animals. Smaller amounts of other grains like barley were also planted. Almost everything a family needed was grown or made on the farm— from food to tools.

THE VIKING AGE BEGINS

The Viking Age is said to have started with the first documented raid on June 8, 793. It was a violent attack on a monastery on an island off the northeastern coast of England. Vikings sailed from Norway and destroyed the church at Lindisfarne by looting it. They also killed the monks who lived there and took some as slaves.

There are many reasons why some Vikings left their northern homes. The climate in Scandinavia was cold and harsh. They wanted to discover new places to trade goods. They were looking to settle in new lands. The Vikings also wanted to find places to raid for valuables.

The Lindisfarne Stone was created to remember those killed in the Viking raid on the monastery. One side of the stone depicts what are believed to be Viking warriors.

For the next three hundred years, the Vikings conducted raids and trade along the North Atlantic coast of Europe and throughout the continent. Vikings journeyed as far as Russia and central Asia. Seafaring groups began to seek their fortunes west of Europe in unexplored lands like Iceland.

TRAVELERS AND TRADERS

The Vikings were excellent seamen who traveled over great distances by boat. Their navigational skills and well-designed ships carried them over seas and down long rivers through many countries. Vikings sailed as far as the Mediterranean and the Far East. Their travels left a lasting impact across the European continent and beyond. Viking boats made it possible to carry large trade goods from near and far.

The Vikings were also known for trading goods peacefully along their travel routes. Most trading was along local routes in Scandinavia. A smaller number of trading routes took the Vikings to international trading centers. There the Vikings bartered with people from Europe, Asia, and Arab countries. Common trade items from Scandinavia included furs, timber, iron, seal fat, walrus tusks, and deer antlers for making combs and needles. From the Far East, the Vikings brought home spices, silk, fruits, and wine.

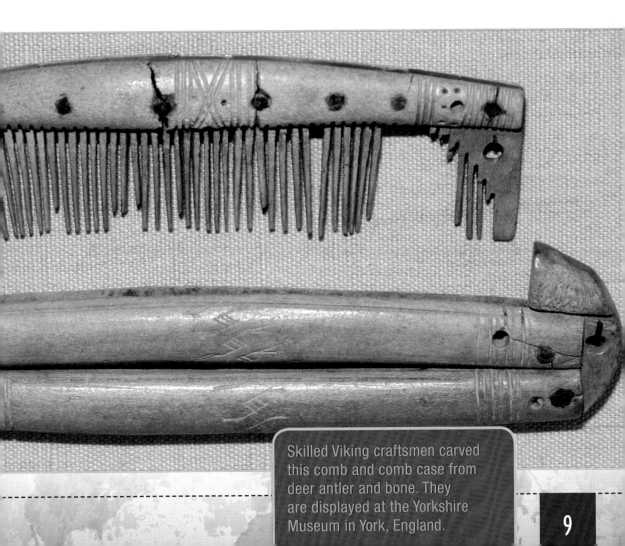

Skilled Viking craftsmen carved this comb and comb case from deer antler and bone. They are displayed at the Yorkshire Museum in York, England.

PILLAGERS AND PLUNDERERS

The Vikings earned their reputation as pillagers and plunderers through hit-and-run raids. They arrived by boat to surprise monasteries and communities along seas or rivers. Early raids were carried out by small groups of Vikings with a few ships. Later raids included fleets of as many as one hundred ships.

The Vikings stole riches and destroyed property before leaving as quickly as they had arrived. Often they kidnapped people and charged ransoms for their return. These activities created great fear among the

citizens of many nations. Later in the Viking Age, the Vikings carried out their raids farther inland from water routes.

Treasures brought back from the raids made some Viking communities wealthy. Some wealth also came from payments made to stop Viking raids. For example, the English paid the Danish Vikings several thousand pounds of silver to prevent them from raiding the English coast.

VIKING WARRIORS

Not all Vikings were raiders or warriors. Only a small number left their farms or trades for weeks at a time to go raiding. Those who did go raiding were feared and called barbaric pirates. Several warriors even gained fame during the Viking Age for their brutal fighting. The most violent warriors were called berserkers.

The main fighting tactic was fearsome hand-to-hand combat. There was no organized fighting. The most commonly used weapon was the spear. Swords were beautifully decorated but were also functional. Battle-axes could inflict great wounds. Archaeologists have uncovered Viking skeletons that show how a man's head could be taken off with a single blow from the blade of a sword.

Viking armor and clothes consisted of leather-covered body shields. Helmets were made from leather or metal, sometimes with a faceguard. Helmets did not have horns. This depiction was invented in the nineteenth century during a time of renewed interest in the Vikings.

Hand-to-hand combat using swords and spears earned the Vikings their reputation as fierce warriors, as depicted in this nineteenth-century print.

VIKING SHIPS

The Vikings developed maritime sailing before they started raiding. They were skilled shipbuilders. Using mostly an axe, they devised and built the longboat. This ship could sail quickly in both shallow and deep water, making it possible to travel by river or sea to many places. During a raid, the Vikings would pull the boat onshore, plunder their target, fight off any resistance, and then quickly get away.

Vikings also built slower boats that carried passengers and cargo. Smaller boats were used for fishing and traveling short distances.

The Vikings were skilled seamen and navigators. They sailed their ships close to land when they could, looking for landmarks to guide them. When that was not possible, the Vikings determined their direction by watching the sun and stars and even the birds. Viking seamen also sailed by paying attention to the direction and color of the sea currents and the wind.

VIKING RELIGIOUS BELIEFS

P agan beliefs and customs, such as the sacrifice of horses, marked the early Viking Age. The Vikings were not yet literate, but they told tales of magic, monsters, giants, dwarfs, and gods. Vikings believed in many gods. Odin was the one-eyed god of wisdom and war. Thor, the god of thunder, was worshipped by seafarers. The Vikings told many myths of his strength and adventures.

The Vikings first heard of Christianity during their raids. The first raid was on the Lindisfarne monastery in England. It was a well-known religious site with educated monks, a large library, and priceless silver and gold objects. The pagan Vikings' attacks on Christian religious places led Christians to call them barbarians.

The Vikings slowly converted to Christianity. They adopted the Christian religion of the lands they raided and settled in. Also, missionaries from other European countries like Germany went to Scandinavia to convert the Vikings to Christianity.

An eleventh-century stone carving from Sweden depicts the three main gods that the early Vikings worshipped: *(from left to right)* Odin, the chief god; Thor, the god of thunder; and Freyr, the god of fertility.

VIKINGS AS ALLIES?

Through the centuries, the Vikings have been best remembered as raiding pirates. Yet, following their invasion of some countries in Europe, the Vikings became accepted and even respected. They even held positions of authority. In eleventh-century Constantinople, Vikings guarded the Byzantine emperors. Slavic peoples hired Vikings to collect taxes and to fight off Turkish invaders.

Many Viking settlements grew from the places they raided and along trade routes they created. Vikings from Sweden traded in the east and intermarried with the local folk

called Rus. This area later became known as Russia.

There is also evidence of Viking raiding and trading in England and Ireland, where Viking place names still exist. Dublin, Ireland, became an important seaport during the Viking Age. Vikings in England helped the local people lead rebellions against the English kings. Even within their own Scandinavian countries, the Vikings had both allies and enemies.

VIKING LIFE

Viking life was centered on providing enough food for a family. Most Vikings were farmers who often struggled to raise animals and crops in a harsh environment. Several generations of one family lived in a longhouse. Some longhouses were small, while others were larger depending on the family's wealth. Viking diets were heavy in meat, fish, and grains. Meals included lamb stew, coarse bread, and buttermilk.

Entertainment in Viking times was simple. Families played games and went to feasts, large gatherings, and markets.

Some Vikings earned a living as craftsmen. They made household items, such as wooden cups and plates, and decorative arts, jewelry, and wood carvings.

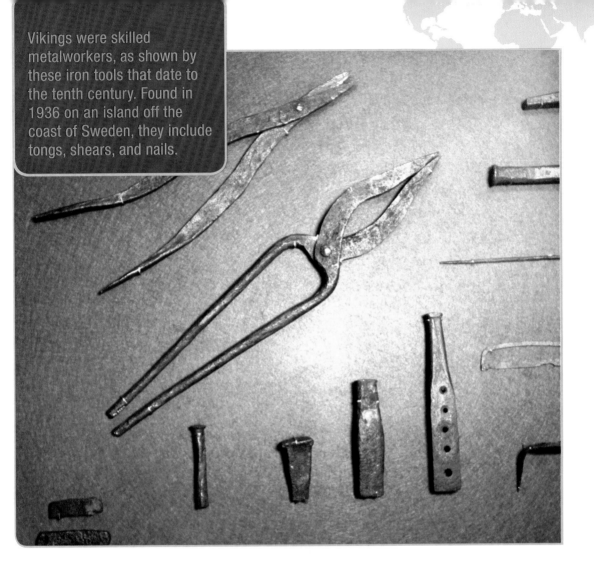

Metalworkers produced tools and weapons such as swords and spears.

The Vikings did not have written laws. Instead, their laws were passed down by word of mouth. They lived by a code of honor, and revenge was part of maintaining a person's honor. Disputes were settled by a fight or a type of duel.

VIKING EXPLORERS BEFORE COLUMBUS

In 1492, Christopher Columbus sailed on the first of four voyages from Spain across the Atlantic. He was searching for a water passage to the Far East when he came across islands in the Caribbean Sea.

The Vikings traveled to the New World nearly five hundred years before Columbus was even born. Viking sagas say they sailed aboard their longboats along the coast of North America without going ashore. Viking ships also sailed off the coast of Newfoundland before they decided to set up

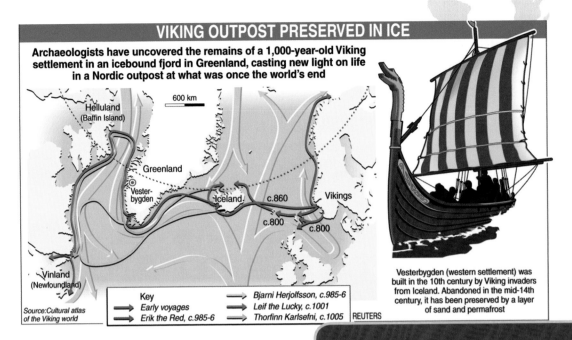

VIKING OUTPOST PRESERVED IN ICE

Archaeologists have uncovered the remains of a 1,000-year-old Viking settlement in an icebound fjord in Greenland, casting new light on life in a Nordic outpost at what was once the world's end

600 km

Helluland
(Baffin Island)

Greenland

Vester-
bygden

Iceland   c.860   Vikings

c.800

c.800

Vinland
(Newfoundland)

Source: Cultural atlas
of the Viking world

Key

Early voyages

Erik the Red, c.985-6

Bjarni Herjolfsson, c.985-6

Leif the Lucky, c.1001

Thorfinn Karlsefni, c.1005   REUTERS

Vesterbygden (western settlement) was built in the 10th century by Viking invaders from Iceland. Abandoned in the mid-14th century, it has been preserved by a layer of sand and permafrost

This map shows the various routes that Vikings traveled across the open seas to explore and colonize Iceland, Greenland, and Newfoundland.

a base camp for more exploration. Explorer Leif Eriksson and his crew spent a winter there before returning home to Greenland. More Vikings briefly explored Newfoundland during the next ten years.

The Vikings did not stay in North America, and their discovery of the continent got lost in Viking legends. Instead, Columbus got the credit because his expeditions started the exploration, colonization, and lasting contact of Europe with the Americas.

FAMOUS VIKINGS:
ERIK THE RED AND LEIF THE LUCKY

Erik the Red was a celebrated Viking explorer. In 986, he founded the first European settlement in Greenland, which lasted nearly five hundred years. Erik's last name was Thorvaldsson. His temper and red hair earned Erik his nickname. He was born in Norway but moved to Iceland after his father was exiled for manslaughter.

In 982, Erik was also exiled for manslaughter for a period of three years. Erik then ventured west from Iceland to a land discovered nearly one hundred years

earlier by a Norwegian sailor. For two years, Erik explored the western and northern parts of this land. It had good pastures, so he called it Greenland. Erik then returned to Iceland and convinced more than four hundred people to follow him back to Greenland. Twenty-five boats set sail, but only fourteen arrived in Greenland to establish new communities.

Leif the Lucky, also called Leif Eriksson, was a son of Erik the Red. He was also a famous Viking explorer. Vikings nicknamed him Leif the Lucky after he rescued another boat during a voyage.

Leif was the first European to travel to the North American continent, beating Christopher Columbus by nearly five hundred years. In about 1000, Leif sailed west from Greenland and explored parts of Newfoundland in Canada. There are two accounts of how he reached the New World. In one story, Leif sailed off course, stumbling across Newfoundland. The other story is that he followed the route of a sailor who had spotted the new land about ten years earlier.

Leif and thirty-five Vikings landed on the coastline of Newfoundland. The group then sailed north and established a settlement they called Vinland, possibly because of the wild

grapes they found there. The Vikings stayed for one winter, living off of plenty of fish and grapes. Legends say that when they returned to Greenland they brought along a boatload of grapes.

Leif Eriksson and his crew sight the North American continent from their longboat. This 1936 oil painting by Norwegian artist Per Krohg is a copy of the original prepared by his father, Christian Krohg, for the Chicago World's Fair in 1893.

VIKING ADVENTURER: THORFINN KARLSEFNI

Thorfinn Karlsefni was a Viking adventurer and trader. In 1010, he set sail from Greenland with three ships and a crew. His destination was the recently discovered Newfoundland. He followed the same route across the northern Atlantic that Leif Eriksson had sailed seven years before.

Karlsefni was in search of riches such as fish, game, timber, and pastures. He also tried to found a settlement there. Conflict with the native people of Newfoundland worsened over time and may be a major reason why the settlement was abandoned. Modern archaeologists have uncovered Viking graves

An archaeologist finds clues about Viking home life in the remains of a Viking house in Newfoundland, Canada.

with arrowheads, indicating there was warfare between the Vikings and native people.

After three years in Newfoundland, Karlsefni, his family, and crew left and returned to his homeland of Iceland. With them was Karlsefni's son, who is believed to be the first European baby born in North America.

NEW WORLD SETTLEMENTS

Greenland was the home of the first European settlement in North America, founded there in about 986. It was a far-northern Viking colony that prospered for nearly five hundred years. More settlers from elsewhere in Scandinavia and Ireland followed the first Viking explorers.

The Vikings lived on hundreds of farms spread out among fjords, which offered protection from weather, intruders, and enemies. Fish and seal meat were plentiful on Greenland. The weather was warm enough to grow corn and barley, which were key ingredients in beer, bread, and porridge—all basic foods in the Viking diet. Later, a cold spell made agriculture difficult,

Large stones mark the ruins of Brattahlid, Erik the Red's estate in the first Viking colony he founded in southwestern Greenland.

as corn could not grow in a shorter warm season. The Vikings also traded with the native people.

Viking communities included several churches overseen by bishops. The settlements on Greenland were never very large. Only about 2,500 to 5,000 people lived there, even after surviving an epidemic of disease.

Newfoundland was the site of the first European settlement founded on the mainland of the North American continent.

The rugged and beautiful terrain of Newfoundland is seen in this photograph of Gros Morne National Park on the west coast of this Canadian island. Vikings often made their homes near fjords.

The Vikings arrived in about 1000, nearly five centuries before Christopher Columbus voyaged to the New World. They may have

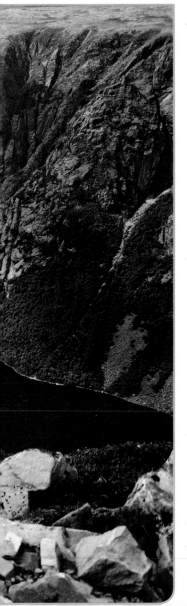

been in search of better farmland. Led by explorer Leif Eriksson, thirty-five men sailed in one ship and landed on the northern peninsula. Near the coast were mountains. Leif named the place "stone slab land."

The explorers then traveled farther north to a place they named Markland, meaning "forestland" in Norwegian. They stayed for one winter in another location they called Vinland, living off of the abundant fish in the rivers and the wild grapes. It is probably because of these grapes, which produced a good wine, that Leif named the place Vinland.

ABANDONING THE NEW WORLD

The Viking colony on the southwestern coast of Greenland lasted for nearly five hundred years. Viking descendants and later settlers lived there from the end of the tenth century to the late fifteenth century. The settlement was abandoned in about 1500. Archaeologists have been able to guess at the reasons the Vikings left Greenland based on the evidence they have found. Several factors may have contributed to why the Vikings left in an organized fashion.

In the mid-thirteenth century, the climate in Greenland turned colder, harsher, and stormy. It became harder to raise farm animals—such as cows, sheep, and goats—in frigid temperatures and with less green pasture for grazing. The Vikings adapted quickly to the decline in farming and ate a diet of more fish and seal meat. However, the Vikings saw themselves as farmers rather than fishermen.

As Greenland's climate changed, the Vikings turned from farming to fishing. This photograph shows a river in Greenland that is teeming with arctic char, a type of cold-water fish.

A slowdown in trade for goods from Greenland, such as sealskins, caused isolation from Europe. Also, the Vikings

Reconstructions of a boat and longhouse made of sod can be seen at L'Anse aux Meadows, the site of the Viking settlement in northern Newfoundland. Archaeologists discovered evidence of this short-lived colony in 1960.

identified more with their roots in Scandinavia than in Greenland.

The Newfoundland outpost of Vinland  was small and had less than one hundred people. It was a short-lived settlement that lasted for only one winter. Leif Eriksson and his band of explorers had little opportunity for trading in that desolate land. They may also have had conflict with the native people. According to legend, when Leif left Vinland he took a boatload of grapes back to Greenland. He never returned to Newfoundland.

Although a permanent settlement was not built in Newfoundland, the Vikings left evidence of their exploration. It is now an archaeological site called L'Anse aux Meadows, which has been recognized as a UNESCO World Heritage Site.

THE VIKING AGE ENDS

The Vikings did not just disappear or die from starvation or disease like some other cultures. There were several reasons why the Viking Age ended.

In 1066, the Battle of Stamford Bridge took place in England. The Viking leader Harald Hardrada launched an invasion to gain more territory, but he was defeated. That battle was followed by the Battle of Hastings. The Vikings defeated the Anglo-Saxons, and William the Conqueror, a Viking descendant, became king of England.

Viking raids slowed down but continued for another one hundred years before they stopped completely. The raids were not as

An eleventh-century tapestry depicts the Battle of Hastings in 1066, marking the Vikings' conquest of England. It is displayed in Normandy, France.

profitable as before and began to have a negative effect on trading with European countries. The climate became colder, freezing the sea-lanes, which made raiding harder. In the Christian countries of Europe, Viking culture and pagan religion became absorbed into the local ways.

A more organized government developed in Scandinavia with the establishment of kingdoms. This form of government had more control over the people, which slowed down the raiding.

THE VIKINGS' LEGACY

The Vikings were pioneers in seafaring exploration. They made a large and lasting impact through their voyages to new lands. Viking raiding and trading brought different cultures together. The Vikings also left evidence of their culture in their settlements throughout Europe and the New World. Trading towns that they founded—like Dublin, Ireland—grew into major cities.

The Vikings left an important mark on our language. Old Norse, the language of the Vikings, was similar to Old English. Many Norse words are used in the modern English language. Words like "wrong," "angry," and "dream" come from Old Norse. Places in

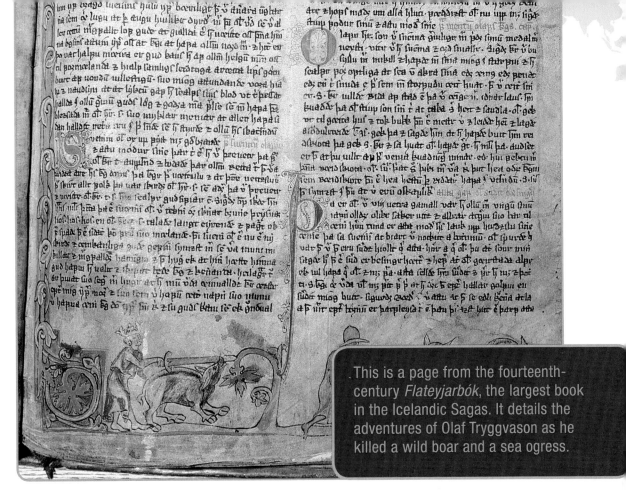

This is a page from the fourteenth-century *Flateyjarbók*, the largest book in the Icelandic Sagas. It details the adventures of Olaf Tryggvason as he killed a wild boar and a sea ogress.

England and Ireland got their names during the time of the Viking raids and settlements. A village outside of London, England, is called Thorpe.

The Vikings wrote the Icelandic Sagas, legends that tell the stories of victorious Viking raids and settlements on Iceland. The Vikings also left behind archaeological evidence of their famous history, such as the longboat.

GLOSSARY

archaeologists People who study earlier cultures.

bartered Exchanged goods without using money.

berserkers Viking warriors who fought in a destructive manner.

cultures Ways of life for different groups of people.

customs Special ways of doing things.

fjords Narrow waterways surrounded by steep cliffs.

frigid Extremely cold temperature.

legacy Something that is handed down from the past.

legends Stories told over time that become accepted as truth.

marauding Creating destruction during a raid.

maritime Anything related to the sea.

monastery A residence occupied by religious persons, such as monks.

navigators People who are skilled in the sailing of ships.

pagan Describes a religion based on many gods.

pillagers People who violently take things.

plunderers People who take valuables in a war or raid.

raids Attacks on a community or group of people.

ransoms The holding by force of a person or thing in exchange for money.

sagas Stories of the lives of the Vikings and Norse people.

sea-lanes Water routes for ships.

Jorvik Viking Centre
Coppergate, York YO1 9WT
England
Website: http://www.jorvik-viking-centre.co.uk
This excavated Viking city, along with a reconstructed
    city and artifacts, showcases what life was like
    there one thousand years ago.

L'Anse aux Meadows National Historic Site
P.O. Box 70
St. Lunaire-Griquet, NL A0K 2X0
Canada
(709) 623-2608 (May–October)
(709) 458-2417 (October–May)
Website: http://www.www.pc.gc.ca/eng/lhn-nhs/nl/
    meadows/index.aspx
The archaeological remains of the first documented
    European settlement in North America, plus a
    recreated sod longhouse, are at this Canadian
    historic site.

Saga Museum
Grandagardi 2
101 Reykjavik
Iceland
Website: http://www.sagamuseum.is
Lifelike exhibits depict stories from the Icelandic

Sagas, including the history of how Iceland was settled and of Viking explorers like Leif Eriksson.

University of Oslo: Museum of Cultural History
Frederiks Gate 2
0164 Oslo
Norway
Website: http://www.khm.uio.no/english
The only complete Viking helmet and the best-preserved Viking ship ever found are displayed at this museum.

Websites

Because of the changing nature of Internet links, Rosen Publishing has developed an online list of websites related to the subject of this book. This site is updated regularly. Please use this link to access the list:

http://www.rosenlinks.com/SEC/viki

Bankston, John. *Leif Erickson* (Junior Biographies from Ancient Civilizations). Newark, DE: Mitchell Lane Publishers, 2013.

Brownworth, Lars. *The Sea Wolves: A History of the Vikings*. London, England: Crux Publishing, 2014.

d'Aulaire, Ingrid, and Edgar Parin d'Aulaire. *Leif the Lucky*. Minneapolis, MN: University of Minnesota Press, 2014.

Higgins, Nadia. *National Geographic Kids Everything Vikings: All the Incredible Facts and Fierce Fun You Can Plunder*. Washington, DC: National Geographic Children's Books, 2015.

Kane, Njord. *The Vikings: The Story of a People*. Yukon, OR: Spangenhelm Publishing, 2015.

Langley, Andrew. *You Wouldn't Want to Be a Viking Explorer!* London, England: Franklin Watts, 2013.

Matthews, Rupert. *DK Eyewitness Books: Explorer.* New York, NY: DK, 2012.

McKinley, Herald. *Vikings: Raiders and Explorers.* New York, NY: Cavendish Square Publishing, 2015.

Potter, William. *The Vikings: The Creative Way to Discover History* (Sticker Histories). London, England: Carlton Kids, 2015.

BIBLIOGRAPHY

Goodrich, Ryan. "Viking History: Facts & Myths." LiveScience.com, May 16, 2013 (http://www .livescience.com).

Keko, Don. "The End of the Viking Age." Examiner.com, May 10, 2011 (http://www.examiner.com).

Klein, Christopher. "Uncovering New England's Viking Connections." *Boston Globe*, November 23, 2013 (http://www.bostonglobe.com).

Lidz, Franz. "The Vikings' Bad Boy Reputation Is Back With a Vengeance." *Smithsonian Magazine*, March 2014 (http://www.smithsonianmag.com).

MacGregor, Neil. "A History of the Viking World—in 10 Extraordinary Objects." *Guardian*, March 3, 2014 (http://www.theguardian.com).

NOVA. "Who Were the Vikings?" PBS, February 8, 2005 (http://www.pbs.org).

Pringle, Heather. "Vikings and Native Americans." *National Geographic*, November 2012 (http://ngm. nationalgeographic.com).

Stockinger, Günther. "Abandoned Colony in Greenland: Archaeologists Find Clues to Viking Mystery." Spiegel Online, January 10, 2013 (http://m.spiegel.de).

Weiner, Eric. "Coming to America: Who Was First?" NPR, October 8, 2007 (http://www.npr.org).

Yale Department of History. "The Vikings: Yale Historian Looks at Myths vs. the History." Yale University, March 8, 2013 (http://history.yale.edu).

INDEX

About the Author

Henrietta Toth is a writer and editor with nearly twenty years' experience in academic publishing. She enjoys reading and writing about early world history as a career as well as a hobby.

Photo Credits